AMAZING Power of ACTIVISM

Lily Dyu

OXFORD
UNIVERSITY PRESS

Great Clarendon Street, Oxford OX2 6DP

Oxford is a registered trade mark of
Oxford University Press in the UK and in certain other countries

Text written by Lily Dyu
Illustrated by Ekaterina Gorelova and Ana Seixas

Designed and edited by Raspberry Books Ltd

First published 2023

British Library Cataloguing in Publication Data:

ISBN 978-0-19-278034-8

1 3 5 7 9 10 8 6 4 2

Printed in China

Paper used in the production of this book is a natural,
recyclable product made from wood grown in sustainable forests.
The manufacturing process conforms to the environmental regulations
of the country of origin.

Acknowledgements

The publisher and authors would like to thank the following for permission to use photographs and other copyright material:

Cover artwork: Ekaterina Gorelova and Ana Seixas; Photos: Pavlo S/Shutterstock; Aleksandr Bryliaev/Shutterstock and author.
Inside artwork: p1: Pavlo S/Shutterstock; p11: Arvind Balaraman/Shutterstock; pp12-13: Asmus Koefoed/Shutterstock; p13(m): Everett Historical/Shutterstock; p13(bgr): Petrov Stanislav/Shutterstock; p19: Soltan Frédéric/Getty Images; p28: American Photo Archive/Alamy Stock Photo; p30(t): American Photo Archive/Alamy Stock Photo; p30(b): Sean Heatley/Alamy Stock Photo; p31: AfriPics.com/Alamy Stock Photo; p33: Georg Kristiansen/Alamy Stock Photo; p40: ftwitty/Getty Images; p41: Joacy Souza/Alamy Stock Photo; p46: Dn Br/Shutterstock; p47: Morphart Creation/Shutterstock; p52: Ruslan Kalnitsky/Alamy Stock Photo; pp52-53: Laura_VN/Shutterstock; p55(t): rahalarts/Shutterstock; p55(m): Mette Holm/Alamy Stock Photo; p55(b): Vectorzz/Shutterstock; p57: Ringo Chiu/Shutterstock; p63: Rich Polk/Getty Images; p65: Science History Images/Alamy Stock Photo; p66: JStone/Shutterstock; p71: Thep Photos/Shutterstock; p72: Michele D'Ottavio/Alamy Stock Photo; p75: TheSilentPhotographer at English Wikipedia (CC BY 3.0); p77 & p78: Neil Atkinson/Alamy Stock Photo; p79: dpa picture alliance/Alamy Stock Photo; p82: PA Images/Alamy Stock Photo; p83: Mark Waugh/Alamy Stock Photo; p84: Action Foto Sport/Alamy Stock Photo.

Artwork by **Ekaterina Gorelova**, **Ana Seixas**, Aaron Cushley, and Raspberry Books.

Every effort has been made to contact copyright holders of material reproduced in this book. Any omissions will be rectified in subsequent printings if notice is given to the publisher.

Contents

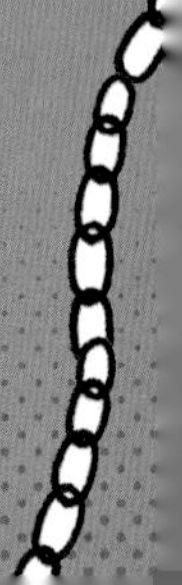

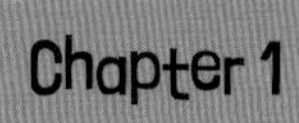

What is Activism?

Activism means taking action to bring about or resist a change, perhaps in the way a country is run or the way people live or are treated.

Activists stand up for what they believe in, whether that's protecting a rainforest, stopping a new mine, or marching against war. Thousands of years ago, striking workers in ancient Egypt were some of the first activists. Today, many of those change-makers are **young people like you!**

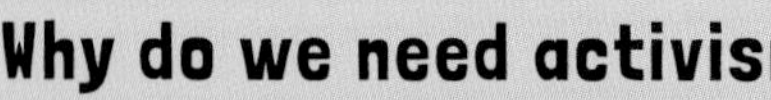

Why do we need activism?

People become activists when they see something happening that they believe is wrong or unfair and want to change it. Not everyone agrees about what is right and wrong, so **campaigns, demonstrations,** and other methods that activists use can be controversial.

Types of activism

There are many different ways to be an activist, and different tactics that activists use to achieve their goals . . .

- working or volunteering for a **POLITICAL PARTY** or activist organization—for example, taking part in elections, organizing **petitions**

- going on **DEMONSTRATIONS**, **rallies** and **MARCHES**, planning **strikes**

- **GETTING IN THE WAY**, for example, by blocking a road or refusing to obey certain laws and rules

- damaging property or attacking people (this is sometimes used—but not recommended!—as a last resort)

An activist's toolkit includes social media, using **hashtags** and sharing pictures and stories, which can reach a lot of people very quickly. Creative tactics include making artworks or writing blogs, songs, books, films, or plays. And the **power of money** can be effective, including the withdrawal of funding and **boycotts**.

We are most powerful when we co-operate, and throughout history ordinary people have come together to change the world. This book is a very short introduction to the activism that has shaped our lives. Read on to discover:

a woman who sat down on a bus and sparked the US civil rights movement

naked cyclists encouraging more people to get on their bikes

thousands of people who marched to collect salt from the sea

how playing football can help save the planet

the artist who risked prison for sharing her drawings

. . . and lots more about the **amazing power of activism.**

Chapter 2

Confronting Colonists

Throughout history, powerful nations have taken over other countries, sometimes to get more land for themselves and their home country, or to make money from the other country's resources (for example, oil, precious stones or metals).

Often, violence has been used to force the **indigenous**, or local, peoples from their homes so that new 'settlers' could move in.

In the 1700s and 1800s, many European countries **formed colonies** in Africa, Asia, North and South America, and the Caribbean.

Speak like an activist

COLONIALISM

This is when one country takes control of another country, making it a colony by occupying it with settlers, ruling it, and making money from its resources.

There are countless tales of activism and **resistance** against colonialism. One in particular—the story of a peaceful man in white robes who defeated a mighty empire—has inspired people around the world.

Gandhi and Indian independence

Mohandas Gandhi was born to a wealthy family in India in 1869, when the country was part of the British Empire. As a child, he learned about Hinduism and Jainism, religions that believe in non-violence. Gandhi became a lawyer and took a job in a British-controlled part of South Africa where one event changed his life for ever—he was thrown off a train carriage that was just for white people.

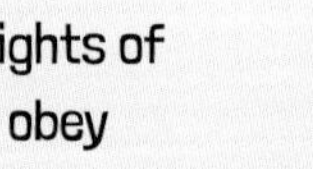

Because of this he began to fight for the rights of Indians in South Africa, telling them to not obey British laws they thought were wrong, while always remaining peaceful. He called his tactic of non-violent activism *satyagraha*, meaning **'devotion to truth'** in the languages Hindi and Sanskrit.

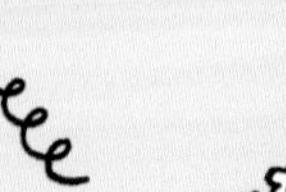

Gandhi believed Indian people should rule India, not the British colonizers. So in 1915 he returned home determined to work for change. He soon became **India's most powerful political leader** and led many peaceful **protests**, encouraging millions of people to boycott British goods and stop entering British courts and schools. He dressed in hand-spun, plain white robes to show he lived as simply as his followers, who were mostly people with little money.

Gandhi's most **powerful protest** was about salt, which everyone needs to stay healthy. The British were forcing Indian people to buy it from British sellers, banning them from making their own, which was cheaper. Gandhi was angry about this, so in September 1930 he set off to walk almost 400 km to collect salt from the sea.

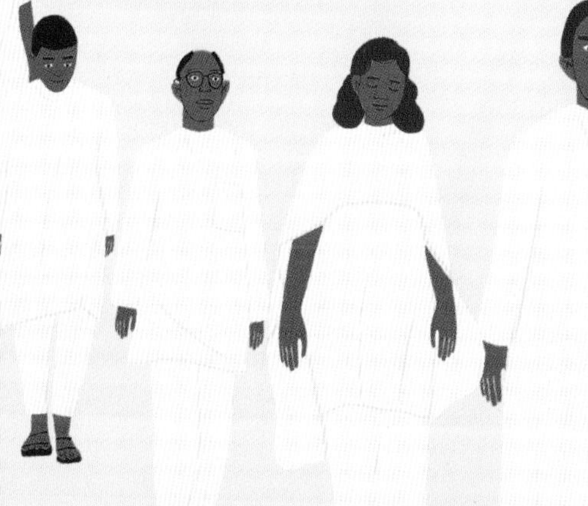

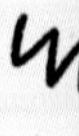

By the time he arrived, **twenty-four days** later, the **Salt March** had grown to **thousands of people.**

Gandhi was arrested for this protest and spent almost nine months in prison, but his actions **inspired thousands** to take part in non-violent civil disobedience and won support around the world. Gandhi and his followers held many more protests in the 1930s and 1940s and he was imprisoned many times. Thanks partly to their activism, British rule in India came to an end in 1947, after 200 years.

As part of the ending of British rule, India was split into two independent countries—India, where people mostly followed the Hindu religion, and Pakistan, where most people were Muslims.

ACTIVIST HERO

MAHATMA GANDHI

Led the Indian people to independence from British rule.

The following year, Gandhi was killed by someone who blamed him for India being divided. He was mourned by his followers, who gave him the name **'Mahatma'**, meaning 'great soul'.

His peaceful protests were so powerful that they changed history and helped end colonialism in India, as well as inspiring millions.

Speak like an activist

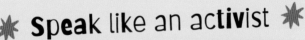

CIVIL DISOBEDIENCE

This means refusing to obey some of a government's laws and demands as part of a protest.

The Slave Trade and the abolitionists

Slavery has existed for thousands of years in many places around the world. Enslaved people are people who are **forced to work** for and obey other people, their enslavers.

From the sixteenth century, European countries continued to colonize other places and encouraged the trade of enslaved people from Africa to grow. This provided free labour for plantations, or large farms, in the European countries' colonies in North and South America and the Caribbean, where crops like sugar, tobacco, and cotton were grown.

Many countries became wealthy from this trade in people, especially Great Britain. In the transatlantic slave trade, ships sailed from British ports to West Africa with products like cloth, brandy, and guns, which they exchanged for captive people. These were usually prisoners of war or people who had been kidnapped by African traders. The captives were transported in **awful conditions** on overcrowded ships across the Atlantic Ocean to North America, where they were sold to enslavers who forced them to work. The empty ships were then loaded with sugar, tobacco, and cotton to sell back in Britain.

Between 1532 and 1832, at least 12 million African people were enslaved and taken to the Americas, of which around **2 million died** on slave ships. Countless more died before beginning the sea journey, and more died working on the plantations. To justify enslaving African people, many enslavers spread the belief that white people were better than other ethnicities, an idea known as white supremacy.

This image shows the terrible conditions on a slave ship.

There was resistance against the slave trade. Some African rulers refused to sell people to the enslavers and occasionally villagers attacked slave ships and set the captives free. There were also **mutinies** on board. Many enslaved people ran away, and there were **rebellions** too—thousands of enslaved people in Saint-Domingue overthrew the French rulers and named their new country Haiti.

Towards the end of the eighteenth century, however, the British public started to turn against the slave trade. Activists called for its abolition, led by a politician called William Wilberforce. These **abolitionists** wrote letters, organized petitions, and asked supporters to boycott sugar (because it was grown on plantations that used enslaved workers). Others went on speaking tours and handed out leaflets describing the dreadful conditions on slave ships and plantations.

One activist, Olaudah Equiano, had been enslaved as a child and sold to a British naval officer. It was sometimes possible for enslaved people to buy their freedom, and Olaudah eventually earned enough money to be set free, aged 21, in 1766.

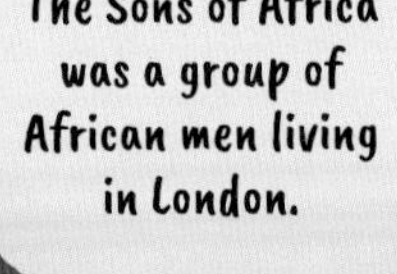
The Sons of Africa was a group of African men living in London.

ACTIVIST HERO

OLAUDAH EQUIANO

A previously enslaved person who campaigned to end slavery.

After this, he helped start the **'Sons of Africa'**, an activist group of African people in Britain, which campaigned against slavery. He also wrote a book about his life and toured the country to share his experiences.

We campaigned to end the slave trade.

Britain's parliament eventually banned the slave trade in 1807. But while this stopped the buying and selling of people, enslaved people continued to work in British colonies for another thirty years. A law to **end slavery** in Britain and its empire, except for India, was finally passed in 1833, but it continued in America for much longer. Sadly, the ideas of white supremacy did not die with slavery, and these continue to lead to **racism**—the belief that one race of people is naturally superior to another.

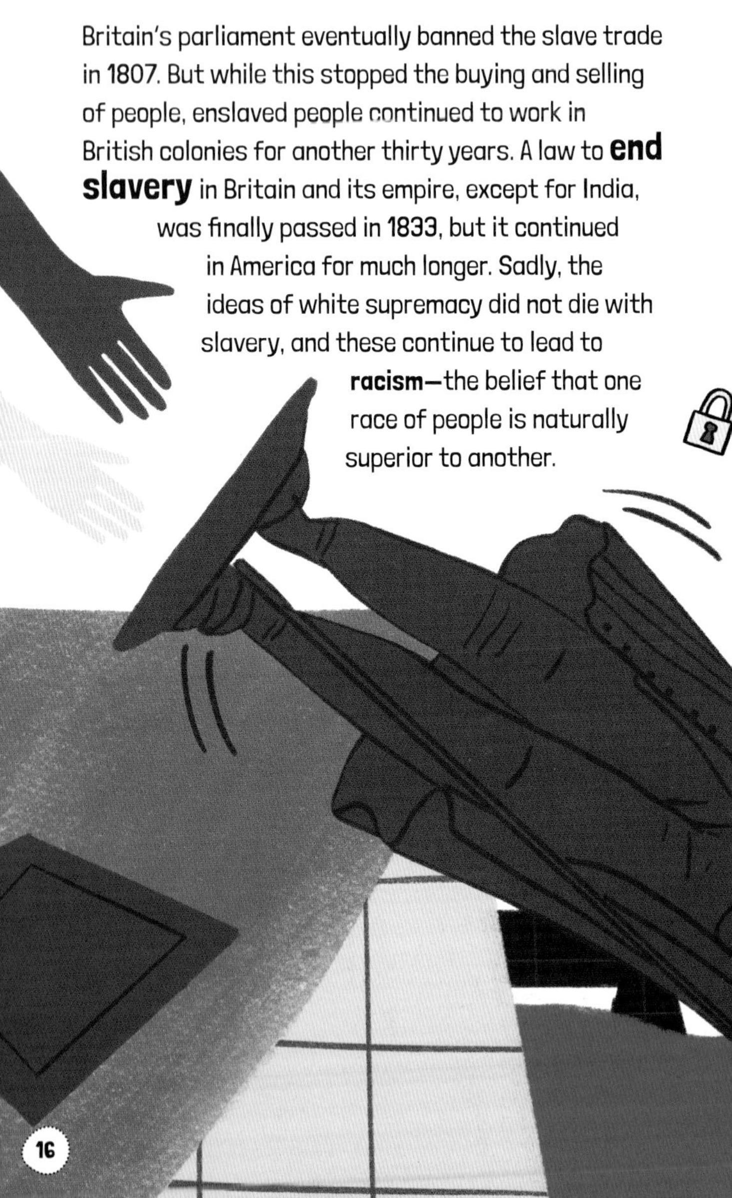

In 2020, protestors in the UK **pulled down a statue** of a slave trader in the city of Bristol, while others called for buildings named after enslavers to be renamed so they do not celebrate people involved in the slave trade. Campaigners today are demanding that Britain's colonial history and the stories of African and Caribbean people in Britain and colonized peoples should be properly taught by schools and universities, known as **'decolonizing the curriculum'**.

The Zapatistas

Chiapas, a state in southern Mexico, has the largest number of indigenous people in the country, and many are descended from the Maya people who once ruled the area. When the Spanish arrived in the 1500s, the region became colonized. The people lost most of their land to settler ranches, where they were forced to work, and **many died from diseases** that arrived with the colonizers as they had no immunity to them.

Mexico became independent from Spain in 1821, but over 150 years later the results of colonialism lived on—most indigenous peoples were poor and suffered racism and **discrimination**. They weren't even allowed to enter Chiapas's capital city. The government did not build schools and hospitals in Chiapas and indigenous peoples were not allowed to vote.

In the 1980s, people in Chiapas started planning to take back land stolen from their Maya ancestors. Unlike Gandhi, the villagers decided to use violence because years of peaceful movements had failed. They formed a **guerrilla** army of ordinary people called the Zapatistas, named after Emiliano Zapata, a Mexican hero, taking up his **rallying** cry of . . .

tierra y libertad
('land and freedom').

Some activists believe that violence is always wrong, while others use violence for their cause as a last resort because all peaceful methods have failed. Sometimes people use violent protest because violence was used against them first.

On New Year's Day 1994, three thousand Zapatistas, one third of them women, began an armed **uprising** against the Mexican government. Wearing face masks, so that no one could recognize them and to represent how they had been made to feel invisible in the past, they demanded self-rule, rights for indigenous peoples, and for land to be shared fairly. Their leader was a mysterious man code-named Subcomandante Marcos, later identified as university professor Rafael Sebastián Guillén Vicente who had moved to Chiapas to help its people. In several days of fighting, around 300 people died.

A mural in support of the Zapatistas

Following the uprising, the two sides held **peace talks** but the government did not agree to all the activists' demands. The Zapatistas decided to set up their own government and build their own schools and hospitals, and in Chiapas today women have a far more equal role in society than in many other parts of Mexico. In recent years, the Zapatistas have given up violence and adopted peaceful tactics. They have gone on marches, organized gatherings for their supporters from around the world, and even put forward a candidate for the Mexican presidential election. Their uprising brought attention to the problems of other groups of indigenous people globally and brought **hope** to other excluded communities.

ACTIVIST HERO

SUBCOMANDANTE MARCOS

(later identified as Rafael Sebastián Guillén Vincente)
Led the Zapatista uprising.

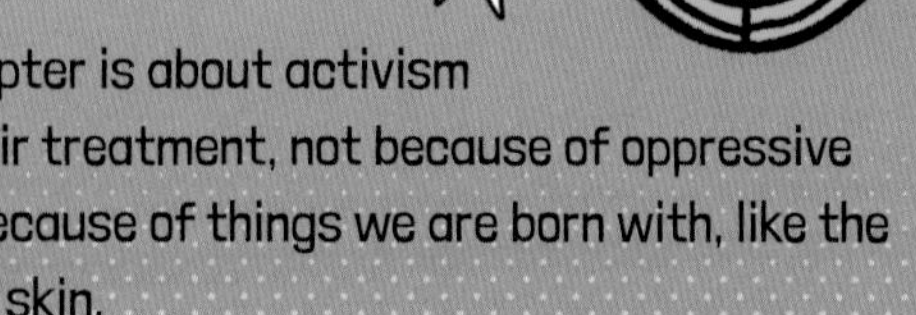

The next chapter is about activism against unfair treatment, not because of oppressive rulers, but because of things we are born with, like the colour of our skin.

Chapter 3

Fighting for Equality

Sometimes people are grouped together based on an aspect of their identity, in order to emphasise their differences and give them fewer rights. These aspects of identity might be gender, ethnicity, class, disability, sexual orientation, religion, age, language, or other parts of their identity. Those people have fought to be treated equally.

In the past, civil rights were granted only to certain people. For example, in most countries, suffrage—the right to vote in political elections—was given only to wealthy men who owned property. This led to **social movements** such as the Chartists in nineteenth century Britain, who were **working-class** men who eventually got the right to vote.

Speak like an activist

SOCIAL MOVEMENT

A social movement is an organized effort by a large group of people to achieve a particular goal, usually a social or political one. This may be to make, resist, or undo a social change.

Through much of history, in many societies, women have not been treated as equals with men. They were thought to be weaker and less intelligent, so they were not allowed to vote. Women knew that this had to change. By voting, they could take part in government and change laws. It is only in the last 150 years that women have been granted the right to vote around the world (and in some countries it is still difficult or dangerous for women to vote). One example of that long struggle took place in late nineteenth and early twentieth century Britain.

Speak like an activist

HUMAN RIGHTS

These are rights that belong to everyone just because they are human, and these include the right to freedom, the right to have shelter and food, and the right not to be treated badly.

CIVIL RIGHTS

These are rights granted to people by their government, for example the right to vote for their leaders, or to be educated.

The suffragettes

In the mid-nineteenth century, groups known as suffragists started to campaign for the women's vote in Britain. Suffragists believed in peaceful methods and sent the first petition for change to parliament in 1865. It was unsuccessful, and the men who voted against it gave reasons such as . . .

In 1903, decades of peaceful talks had not achieved results, so an activist named Emmeline Pankhurst started a new group called the Women's Social and Political Union, also known as the **suffragettes.** She believed that only extreme actions would make people change their minds about votes for women, and this was summed up in the motto,

'Deeds not words'.

The suffragettes called on followers to take part in acts of **violence and civil disobedience** and their tactics included planting bombs, setting buildings on fire, breaking windows, and disrupting speeches. Many disagreed with their methods, but Emmeline argued that violence made headlines, drawing attention to their cause.

ACTIVIST HERO

EMMELINE PANKHURST

Founded the suffragettes in Britain.

Almost 1,000 suffragettes, including Emmeline, were arrested and sent to prison where they went on **hunger strike** (a tactic where people protest by refusing to eat).

The First World War began in 1914 and Emmeline helped organize women to take on many of the jobs done by the men who were fighting. After the war, the contribution that women had made changed public opinion towards the women's vote. Finally, in 1918, over fifty years after the first petition, middle- and upper-class women over 30 were given the vote. Ten years later, in 1928, just a few weeks after Emmeline died aged 69, this was reduced to age 21, in line with all men.

In the nineteenth and twentieth centuries, women faced similar battles all over the world. New Zealand was the first place to grant women the **right to vote** in 1893, and over the next century almost every country followed, with the most recent being Saudi Arabia in 2015. Today, Vatican City is the only country that does not allow women to vote—though barriers still exist in many places.

The US civil rights movement

IN DECEMBER 1955, ROSA PARKS WAS RIDING HOME ON A BUS IN MONTGOMERY, ALABAMA, USA.
Give up your seats in the coloured section, the white section's full!
No.

Rosa was travelling on a segregated bus, where Black and white passengers had to sit in separate sections. Laws of **segregation** in the USA at the time stopped Black people using facilities reserved for white people, such as schools and parks, or even drinking-water fountains, and the facilities for Black people were always worse than those for white people.

Even though slavery had ended in 1865 in America, decades later, Black people still **did not have equality.** Local leaders made it hard for them to vote by forcing them to pass tests first. And while northern states did not have segregation, many Black people living there faced racism and discrimination and had lower-paid jobs and worse housing than white people.

Rosa Parks' actions were part of the growing US civil rights movement—the campaign through the 1950s and 1960s for equal rights and **racial justice** for Black Amcricans.

Inspired by her bravery, activists organized the **Montgomery Bus Boycott** where Black people refused to travel on buses, causing the bus company to lose lots of money. This lasted over a year and eventually led to a ban on segregation on buses.

RACIAL JUSTICE

This means treating people from different races fairly and equally.

ACTIVIST HERO

ROSA PARKS

Refused to give up her bus seat to a white man and sparked the US civil rights movement.

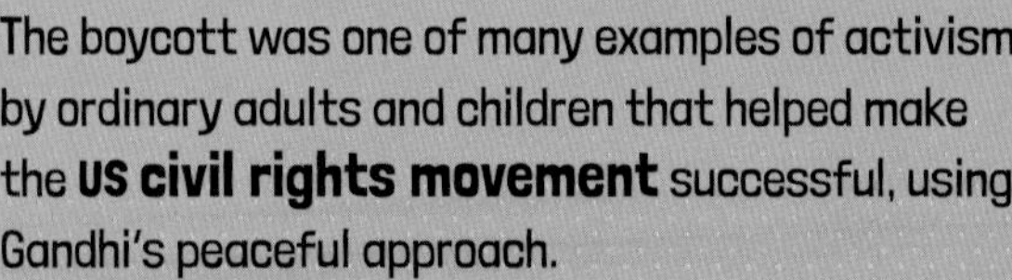

The boycott was one of many examples of activism by ordinary adults and children that helped make the **US civil rights movement** successful, using Gandhi's peaceful approach.

In 1957, nine Black teenagers took up their right to attend a previously white-only school at Little Rock, Arkansas despite angry demonstrations. The 1960s saw Black Americans stage **sit-ins** in white-only restaurants. Black and white activists took **'freedom rides'** together on buses to protest against segregated bus stations, resulting in them being beaten up by white demonstrators. Black singers wrote popular protest songs, and the largest demonstration saw a quarter of a million people in the **'March on Washington for Jobs and Freedom'** to hear civil rights leader Martin Luther King give a famous speech.

Martin Luther King's speech is often known as his 'I Have a Dream' speech.

I have a dream that my four little children will one day live in a nation where they will not be judged by the colour of their skin but by the content of their character.

Thanks to the US civil rights movement, segregation, and also discrimination in voting and housing were eventually banned. However, despite these laws, Black Americans still face racism and discrimination today.

ACTIVIST HERO

MARTIN LUTHER KING

Led the US civil rights movement.

Nelson Mandela and the anti-apartheid movement

An old apartheid sign.

For most of the twentieth century, South Africa lived under apartheid, which means 'apartness' in the language of Afrikaans. Most South Africans are Black, Asian, or mixed race—but due to colonialism white people were in charge of government and set up the unfair laws of apartheid.

Under this system, people were **divided by their ethnicity** and forced to live separately from each other. There were separate parks, restaurants, beaches, buses, hospitals, schools, and toilets for the different ethnicities. Apartheid was used to keep the best land for white people and to deny basic rights to everyone else. Black, Asian and mixed-race people had to **carry special passes** to travel outside their areas, were not allowed to marry white people, and were banned from voting. Black people were the poorest of all.

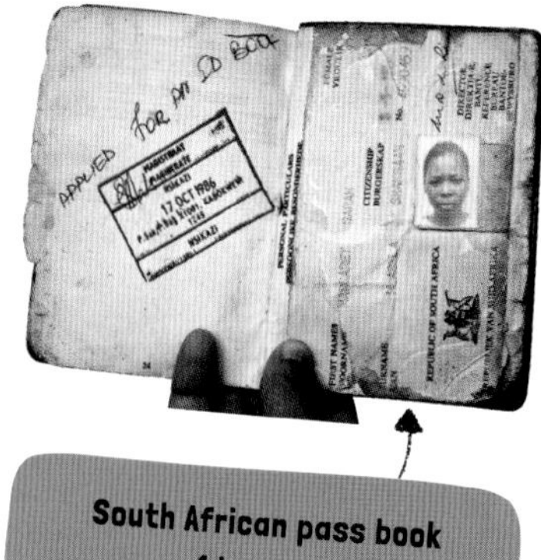

South African pass book (dompas)

Nelson Mandela was a leader in the **African National Congress (ANC)**, an organization fighting for equal rights for all South Africans, regardless of their ethnicity or skin colour. Initially the ANC tried to bring about change peacefully, but after the government shot nearly 250 Black protestors at a demonstration organized by the Pan-Africanist Congress (PAC), they decided they had no choice but to use violent tactics. Mandela helped to set up a guerrilla army called 'Spear of the Nation'. At first, they used **sabotage**, blowing up electricity pylons and buildings, to try to avoid hurting people. But later, the group went on to kill hundreds of people.

They felt they were right to do so because the society was so unfair and the government was using **terrible violence** against them. Many Black people also went on strikes and demonstrations. To try to control them, the government banned the ANC and other political parties.

Nelson Mandela was willing to die for his beliefs, but when he was captured, instead of facing the death penalty, he was imprisoned by the government.

Despite global protests against apartheid and calls for his release, he spent nearly thirty years behind bars. Other countries were boycotting South African goods, which made the country poorer, while violence and unrest by Black people threatened to lead to a civil war.

ACTIVIST HERO

NELSON MANDELA

South Africa's first Black president, who led the anti-apartheid movement.

For these reasons, in February 1990, the President of South Africa, F W de Clerk unbanned the other political parties and set Nelson Mandela free. After leaving prison, Mandela worked with the president to bring change and **peace** in South Africa. Apartheid ended in 1994 and all people of colour were given the right to vote. In that year's election, Nelson Mandela became the first Black president of South Africa, and, with de Clerk, he was awarded the 1993

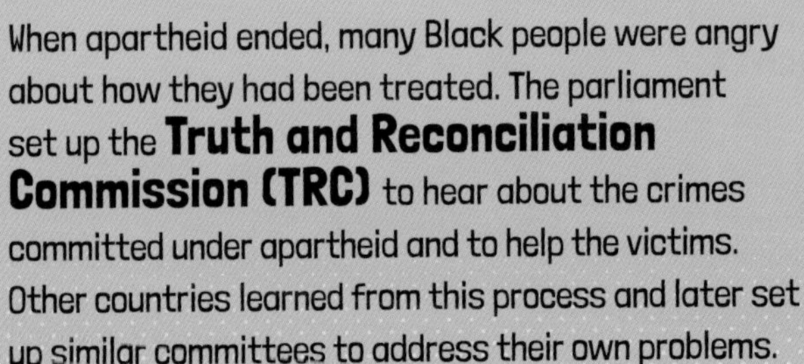

Nobel Peace Prize.

When apartheid ended, many Black people were angry about how they had been treated. The parliament set up the **Truth and Reconciliation Commission (TRC)** to hear about the crimes committed under apartheid and to help the victims. Other countries learned from this process and later set up similar committees to address their own problems.

Stonewall riots and gay rights

In many parts of the world in the past, if you had sexual relationships with people of the same sex as yourself **you could be put in prison**, or even executed. In some places this is still true today.

In twentieth century America, there were laws against being gay. Gay people had to keep their sexuality secret otherwise they might be attacked or refused jobs or housing.

Activists tried to change those laws, but they had little success until the events of 28 June 1969 in **New York City.**

STONEWALL MEANS
FIGHT BACK!
SMASH GAY OPPRESSION!
GAY RIGHTS

The Stonewall Inn was a bar in New York City popular with gay people. Police regularly raided the building to arrest customers because being gay in public was against the law, but that night, for the first time, customers **rose in anger** against years of unfair treatment. There was a riot involving nearly 400 people who fought back against police, threw stones and bottles, and damaged cars and buildings until the police left. Some protestors and police were hurt, but the gay community felt empowered by their successful resistance and the protests continued for several nights.

The riots were an important turning point in the lives of gay people, who began to speak out openly. In America, a group called the Gay Liberation Front formed to **fight for gay rights.**

WE DEMAND JUSTICE
GAY POWER

Newspapers were launched for the gay community and on the first anniversary of the riots, hundreds of protestors marched past the Stonewall Inn in the first Gay Pride March.

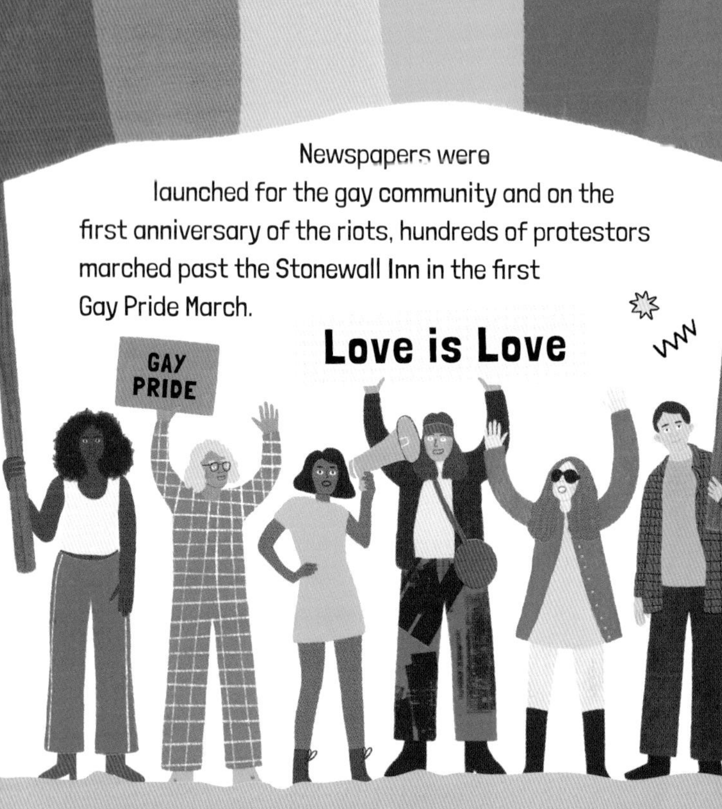

Love is Love

These marches have spread to many countries and since the Stonewall riots, thanks to campaigning by activists, laws have been created in many countries to help protect **LGBTQ+** people from discrimination.

This chapter has been about how activists have fought for equal rights. In the next we'll hear how they have fought against terrible working conditions—and won.

Chapter 4

Workers' Rights

When wealthy people have the power to control workers' lives, workers are often treated very badly so that the business or landowner can make more money. Workers have protested, and gradually their conditions and pay have improved.

The Peasants' Revolt

Life was hard for England's poor in the Middle Ages. Most lived as serfs, who were poor people working on the land, tied to lords under the **feudal system** with no freedom to leave. The lords could even decide who they were allowed to marry!

The feudal system pyramid

KING

LORDS

KNIGHTS

SERFS

Religion was very important, and the **Christian Church** was powerful and rich. The Church and the lords earned money from the work the peasants did for them.

A plague known as the **Black Death** had killed off half the population by 1353. Serfs were in short supply and the lords made them work harder. Things got even worse in 1381, when the government announced a tax to help pay for a war against France.

When a tax collector arrived at a village in Essex to force people to pay the tax, it set off a rebellion amongst poor people, who refused to obey. Soon villagers in both Essex and Kent were in **revolt**—violently protesting against the people in power. Both groups of rebels marched to London where, joined by many of London's poor, they destroyed the houses of government ministers.

On 15 June, the 14-year-old king, Richard II, met the rebels' leader Wat Tyler, who explained their demands. The rebels wanted the Church to give its wealth to the poor, fairer laws, and everyone to be free and equal.

King Richard agreed to some of their demands—but only after William Walworth, Lord Mayor of London, had killed Wat Tyler. The rebels weren't happy but went home. King Richard had been lying—later his troops toured the villages, hanging anyone who had taken part in the uprising.

The uprising was defeated, but the wealthy lords of England had been given a shock—their workers might rise up if they carried on treating them badly. They began to give the serfs more **freedom and money.** Eventually, after a very long time, all the peasants' demands were met.

Yes I agree to all your demands!

Hahaha!

Trade unions

Through the Middle Ages in Europe, growing numbers of people worked in towns in jobs such as baker, blacksmith, and butcher. Guilds started to form, which were **clubs of craftspeople** who controlled the practice of their craft and trained younger people. There were many types of guilds, including weavers and dyers in the wool trade, and masons and architects in the building trade. As jobs moved to factories in the industrial age of the 1800s, the guilds grew into 'trade unions' which **fought for workers' rights.** Those groups are still very active today.

A **trade union** is a group of workers who negotiate pay, hours, benefits, and working conditions, often **using strikes** to achieve their demands.

They have ensured we have things like sick pay, holiday pay, and maximum working hours.

Activists use placards, banners, and signs to get their messages across.

One of their first victories was **weekends off** for workers.

The two-day weekend is a recent thing in most countries. In 1929 in America, for example, a trade union for clothing workers was the first union to demand and receive an agreement for a five-day working week, instead of six. The rest of the country slowly followed, but it was not until 1938 that it became law. From the 1940s to the 1960s, lots of other countries also introduced a two-day weekend, especially as many businesses wanted their workers to follow the same patterns wherever they were in the world.

These protesters in Brazil are demanding better working conditions.

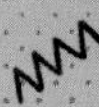

Workers' rights today

Activists have struggled hard to improve workers' lives, but today conditions are getting worse for many people who do not have the right to holiday and sick pay or the security of fixed working hours. **Migrant** workers may not have the rights many others enjoy, while increasing numbers of young people are doing work without pay as interns to gain experience. Around the world, many warehouse workers are unhappy with their working conditions. For all these reasons, activism for workers' rights is **fighting new battles in the twenty-first century.**

People's dissatisfaction with their work and lives can lead to uprisings, strikes, and protests, as we have seen in this chapter,

but they could all form part of an even bigger change—

Chapter 5

Revolution: Power to the People

During a period called the Enlightenment, which started in Europe in the 1700s, people began to believe that everyone was equal and should all have the same rights. But they realized that the only way to make their government equal and fair was to get rid of it and begin again—in other words, start a revolution. These beliefs helped shape one of the best-known revolutions of all . . .

The French Revolution

In Paris, on 14 July 1789, a crowd of people stormed the infamous Bastille prison looking for gunpowder and weapons while releasing all the prisoners. This moment was the start of the French Revolution, an event that went on to inspire others living in unfair societies around the world.

Delicious macarons!
What are they worried about? If they don't have enough bread, let them eat cake!

In the 1700s, the French king, Louis XVI ruled the country with absolute, or unlimited, power. Louis and Queen Marie-Antoinette, the wealthy nobles (people of high social class), and the Church were unpopular because they all enjoyed **lavish lifestyles** while the rest of the country was suffering in poverty. France had spent too much money on wars and there had been years of poor harvests, cattle disease, and high bread prices. Poor people in towns and cities were unhappy about paying taxes when their lives were so hard.

Speak like an activist

REVOLUTION

A revolution involves large masses of people taking power from a government that treats its people unfairly. It usually happens quickly and begins with a rebellion.

At the time, many groups wanted change. The new ideas of the Enlightenment were becoming popular. **Ordinary workers were tired** of working for rich landowners. A new middle class of wealthy city people, known as the Bourgeoisie, wanted more power.

The unfair society eventually led to strikes and a violent uprising in Paris with riots, looting, and the storming of the Bastille. All around France, poor people **burned the castles** of the wealthy landowners, while some regions formed new governments, inspired by the events in the capital. The slogan of the revolution was . . .

Liberté,
egalité,
fraternité!

. . . meaning **freedom, equality,** and **fraternity** (or friendship and support between people).

For the first time, ordinary people had taken control and formed their own government while the king's powers were stripped away. In August 1789, the new government declared that all people are born free and have equal rights and that peasants no longer had to farm nobles' land for no pay. It also took property away from the Church and gave most men the right to vote (though not women).

Initially, the new leaders let the king remain on the throne, but in September 1792 France changed its form of government from a kingdom to a republic (where power is held by the people who elect a president, rather than by a king or queen) and in 1793 Louis and Marie-Antoinette were executed using a new machine called

the guillotine.

It's estimated that up to **40,000 people were executed or murdered** for being against the revolution. This period was called the

Reign of Terror.

The republic didn't last, and France was ruled by a king again for a time, but the country finally became a republic for good in 1871. The French Revolution was one of the most **violent and bloody** in history, but it succeeded in giving power to the people, overturning the king, and ending the unfair society. In addition, the ideas behind the French Revolution spread to many other places.

Fall of the Berlin Wall

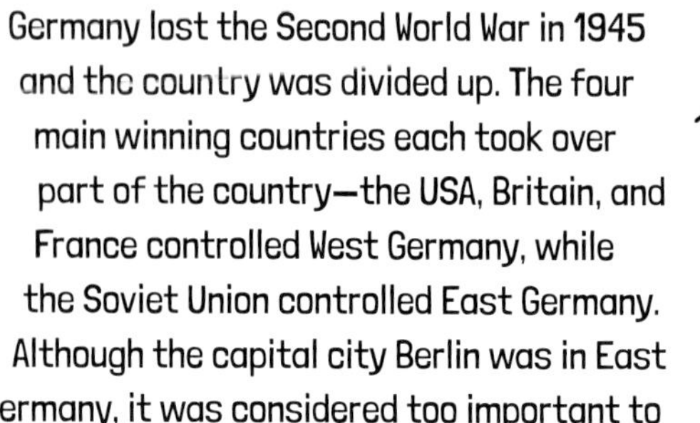

Germany lost the Second World War in 1945 and the country was divided up. The four main winning countries each took over part of the country—the USA, Britain, and France controlled West Germany, while the Soviet Union controlled East Germany. Although the capital city Berlin was in East Germany, it was considered too important to be controlled by just the Soviet Union, so it was also divided in two. **West Berlin** became the capital of West Germany, while **East Berlin** was the capital of East Germany.

Under Soviet rule, East Germany was ruled by a **dictatorship**, which controlled the lives of its people using secret police and stopped them from travelling freely or speaking out. Many wanted to leave and between 1949 and 1961, about **3.5 million** East Germans fled to West Germany. In 1961 the East German government tried to stop people escaping into West Berlin by building a concrete wall through the middle of the city.

Suddenly people in East Berlin were **separated from friends and family** on the other side. By the 1980s the Berlin Wall extended 45 km through Berlin and stretched a further 120 km all around West Berlin.

Soldiers guarded the wall on the East German side, but many people still tried to escape, hiding in the boots of cars, or under seats.

Some tried to leave using

secret tunnels,

ziplines,

and even a homemade

hot air balloon!

Around 5,000 people managed to make their way into West Berlin, but another 5,000 were caught and almost 200 people were killed as they tried.

Speak like an activist

DICTATORSHIP

In a dictatorship, the government's power is in the hands of a single person who rules the nation. Other political parties are not allowed, and the people take no part in politics and have little freedom to say what they want.

In the city of Leipzig, a weekly meeting of 'prayers for peace' grew into an activist group that organized demonstrations to demand **democracy** (or free elections), freedom to travel, and free speech. In October 1989, thousands of protestors risked their lives by demonstrating in Leipzig's streets, many carrying placards saying **'Wir sind das volk'** (We are the people). The police were outnumbered, so they did not use force against the crowds. This inspired other protests around the country that helped to force the East German government out of power later that year.

Speak like an activist

DEMOCRACY

Democracy is rule by the people— a type of government where people can take part in the decisions that affect the way their country is run.

On 9 November 1989, officials opened the country's borders with West Germany.

There were amazing scenes at the Berlin Wall where **thousands of people celebrated** by climbing on it, hammering chunks from it, and flooding through to the other side. Soon after this, the wall was torn down and the whole country was reunited, bringing democracy to East Germany.

To this day, the fall of the Berlin Wall is a symbol of Germany becoming **one country** again and the end of the Cold War, the long-running rivalry between the two biggest powers in the world at the time—the USA and the Soviet Union. It showed how people coming together peacefully to demand their freedom can bring about change.

Under oppressive governments, like the one in East Germany, people have found **creative ways to protest** when speaking out is banned. In the 2020 election in Belarus, many people believed that the president, Alexander Lukashenko, had cheated to stay in power. After he banned demonstrations and the red and white flag of the opposition party, women protested by lining roads and **handing out flowers**

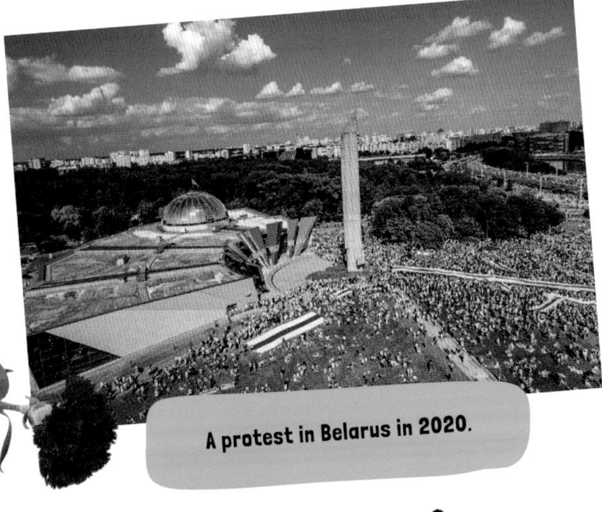

A protest in Belarus in 2020.

to passing drivers. Choirs came together to sing a new protest anthem. Communities held courtyard concerts while groups gathered to dance and exercise outside. And people wore red and white, and carried striped umbrellas.

Revolution today

Revolutions have been enormously varied. Some were non-violent, while others led to terrible civil wars. Some gave people democracy and freedom, while others ended with brutal dictatorships. But as long as leaders treat their people badly, people will continue to risk their lives by trying to overturn their governments to create a fairer society.

Yet even in democratic countries, not everyone is treated fairly and equally. We will find out about that next . . .

Chapter 6

Going Global: Rights for Everyone

In the twentieth century Black people, women, and gay people gained civil rights through activism. Today, activists are still fighting to end discrimination against these groups. These social movements have also become 'intersectional' as they look at the needs of all their members. As a result, there are more groups working for equal rights than ever before.

Speak like an activist

INTERSECTIONALITY

Intersectionality is the idea that because people have different, overlapping identities, such as gender, ethnicity, class, disability, sexual orientation, or age, discrimination may affect them differently. An intersectional social movement recognizes that discrimination is not the same for everyone.

Black Lives Matter

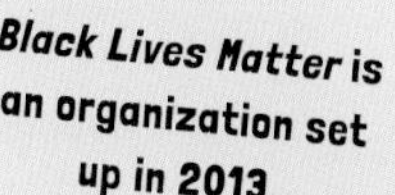

Black Lives Matter is an organization set up in 2013.

During 2020, a wave of Black Lives Matter (BLM) protests spread around the globe, triggered when African American **George Floyd** was murdered by a police officer who kneeled on his neck for nine minutes and 29 seconds. It came on top of the killings of several other Black American people by police.

The Black Lives Matter movement began after teenager Trayvon Martin was shot and killed in 2012, which led to angry protests. An activist named Patrisse Cullors created the hashtag **#BlackLivesMatter,** which spread across social media (the hashtag was used nearly 12 million times on Twitter in its first three years). She and her friends Alicia Garza and Opal Tometi turned BLM into an organization whose goals are to fight racism against Black people and to end **police brutality.** It was set up as an intersectional movement from the start, placing marginalized Black groups at its centre, and today it has groups in many countries.

ACTIVIST HEROES

PATRISSE CULLORS, ALICIA GARZA, AND OPAL TOMETI

Started the Black Lives Matter movement.

At BLM protests, people often kneel on one knee, a gesture called 'taking the knee'. Symbolic gestures like this can be used as powerful messages of protest because everyone knows what the message is straight away. Symbols of protest help people identify a shared cause and help us to remember important moments in history. In Chile, people banged pots and pans to protest about food shortages and rationing (a type of protest called *cacerolazo*). The Umbrella Movement in Hong Kong started when student demonstrators held up umbrellas to protect themselves from pepper spray used by the police. And in Thailand, anti-government protesters use a three-finger salute which stands for freedom, equality, and brotherhood.

Taking the knee began in 2016, when former San Francisco 49ers footballer Colin Kaepernick first protested against racism and police brutality by kneeling during the American national anthem, saying

Colin Kaepernick

that while he loved America, he could not be proud of a flag for a country that oppressed Black people and other ethinic groups. His beliefs led to him losing his job while the National Football League (NFL) banned players from kneeling during the national anthem.

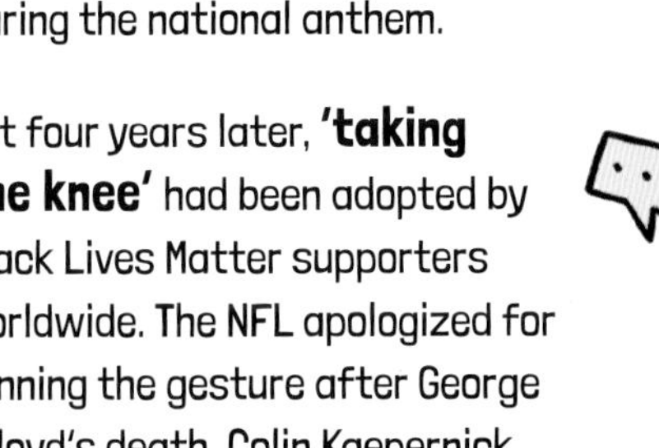

But four years later, **'taking the knee'** had been adopted by Black Lives Matter supporters worldwide. The NFL apologized for banning the gesture after George Floyd's death. Colin Kaepernick has become a committed activist against racism and he has inspired countless others to stand up for what they believe in.

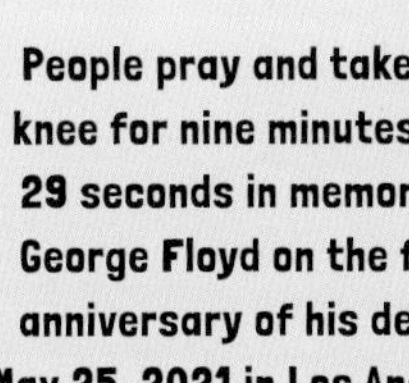

People pray and take the knee for nine minutes and 29 seconds in memory of George Floyd on the first anniversary of his death, May 25, 2021 in Los Angeles.

Black Lives Matter has helped identify the need for justice and change. American cities have begun to look at how to change unfair police practices and the movement has caused people to talk about how to make the world a fairer and equal place for all ethnic groups.

Children's rights

Around the world, some children have such tough lives that they don't really have a childhood. They might be forced to work, marry young, miss out on school, go hungry, experience poor health, or not have a proper roof over their heads.

There are things everyone needs, such as **food and shelter,** and these are human rights that apply to everyone—but children have additional needs too. These include **love, protection, and support** as they grow and learn. Because of this, in 1989 the **United Nations (UN)** created a list of children's rights made up of those extra needs—the UN Convention on the Rights of the Child—and most governments of the world have promised to stick to this list. It includes the right to education and play, and the right to protection from violence and harm in childhood.

Children's rights activists work on behalf of young people everywhere, raising awareness about children's living conditions and working to make positive changes. Many of these activists are young people themselves, inspired to take action on problems that have affected them directly.

Mayra Avellar Neves grew up in Rio de Janeiro in Brazil, in a favela—an area of poor, overcrowded housing. Shootings between gangs and the police killed many adults and children each year. When she was 11 years old, the favela became so **dangerous** that schools and clinics had to be closed.

Mayra eventually found another school she could attend, but she wanted other children in her favela to be able to go to school too. When she was 15, she organized a children's 'Peace March Against Violence', demanding that gangs and police stopped firing near the schools. The **gangs and police took notice** and stopped the violence near schools, which also allowed people to travel to work safely.

ACTIVIST HERO

MAYRA AVELLAR NEVES

Campaigns against violence in Brazilian favelas.

A year later, Mayra led an even bigger 'Walk for Peace' to protest against favela violence and to highlight the fact that children who grow up in favelas are excluded from many parts of life in Brazil.

Rather than move away, Mayra stayed in the favela, determined to **make life better for children** who live there. She has helped the children get online, used theatre to stand up for children's rights, and helped make a documentary that has been shown around the world. In 2007, she was awarded the International Children's Peace Prize for her activism.

Disability rights

A disability is a physical or mental condition that makes life harder for people because society often does not meet their needs. Disability activists campaign for the rights of **disabled people to be included** in every aspect of life, and for their needs to be met. In South Africa, Michaela Mycroft, or **Chaeli** as she likes to be known, is a passionate campaigner for disabled children, fighting to ensure that they are included and have the same opportunities as non-disabled children.

Chaeli has **cerebral palsy,** a brain condition which has affected the use of her arms and legs, and she has been a wheelchair user all her life. Her activism began when she was 9 years old, when she and her friends started the Chaeli Campaign to raise money for a motorized wheelchair to give her more independence. They sold handmade cards and decorated plant pots, as well as asking for donations. After quickly reaching their target, they decided to continue fundraising to provide more disabled South African children with the equipment they needed. Since then, the Chaeli Campaign has grown into a charity that supports disabled children all over the world.

Chaeli likes to focus on things she can do rather than those she can't, and loves taking on challenges to raise awareness of disability rights. She has reached the **top of Kilimanjaro**, the highest mountain in Africa. She completed the 90-km **Comrades Marathon**, after campaigning for rules to be changed so wheelchair users could take part, and she and her dance partner, Damian Michaels, are world champions in wheelchair ballroom dancing.

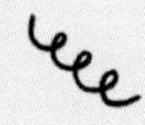

ACTIVIST HERO

MICHAELA MYCROFT

Campaigns for equal rights for disabled children.

Chaeli Mycroft taking part in the Comrades Marathon

People with disabilities constantly battle stereotypes and misconceptions about what they can do. In 1970s America, **Judy Heumann** was turned down for a teaching job because of her disability, but she fought a court case which overturned the decision and became the first teacher in New York using a wheelchair. In 1977, Judy played a key role in a **24-day sit-in protest** that helped to get the *Americans with Disabilities Act* implemented. Her tireless work for disability rights continues and she acted as an advisor to Barack Obama when he was President.

In the past, disabled people have been excluded from many areas of life, for example, because of access to buildings and public transport, but activists **have brought change.** In 1995, in Delhi, India, hundreds of disabled people demonstrated against their unfair treatment. Their protest helped to make it illegal for employers, shops, restaurants, and schools to discriminate against disabled people, which means changing attitudes and adapting buildings and equipment to ensure this doesn't happen.

ANGRY
WOMEN
Will Change
the World

Women's rights

Despite having the right to vote, in many places women still struggle to be treated equally to men, whether it's winning equivalent

prizes in sports or being equally represented in parliament. In North America and Europe in the 1960s, a new women's rights movement began called women's liberation or **feminism.** The groups involved were mainly white, and the movement has been criticized for excluding women of colour. It aimed to free women from inequalities in relation to men, and it helped make birth control available to more women, which gave them **greater freedom** over when they had children and allowed more women to have careers.

A women's liberation march

But women faced unfairness at work too. They were often paid less than men, or forbidden to take jobs (such as construction jobs) that only men were allowed to do, or even forced to give up their jobs when they got married. Women's rights activists have worked to ensure laws treat women and girls the same as men and boys in the workplace and in education.

Women's Rights are Human Rights

ACTIVIST HERO

MALALA YOUSAFZAI

Nobel Prize winner and campaigner for girls' education.

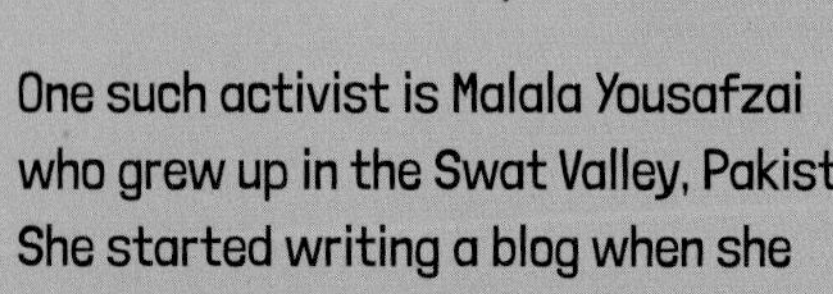

One such activist is Malala Yousafzai who grew up in the Swat Valley, Pakistan. She started writing a blog when she was 12, speaking up for girls who had been **banned** from going to school by the Taliban, a political and religious group. Malala's activism made her a target and she was **shot by a Taliban soldier**, but survived. Today she still campaigns for girls' education and was awarded the Nobel Peace Prize, the youngest winner ever.

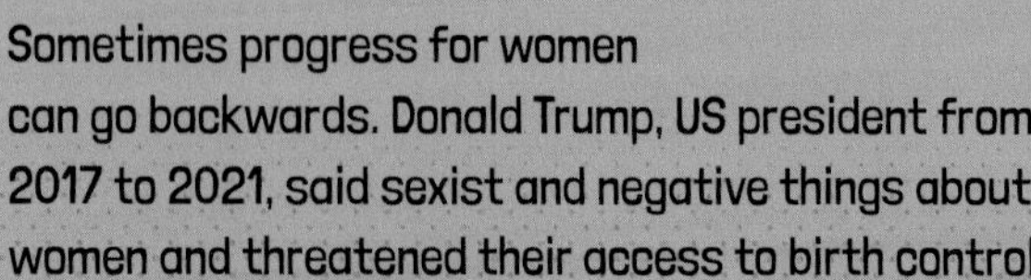

Sometimes progress for women can go backwards. Donald Trump, US president from 2017 to 2021, said sexist and negative things about women and threatened their access to birth control

and abortion. But the 2017 Women's March saw millions of women marching in Washington and around America in protest.

Later that year, the **#MeToo** movement spread globally when women and girls started using the hashtag on social media to share their experiences of being treated badly by men. Women find the **courage to speak** out when they learn they are not alone, and it shows men that they cannot rely on women and girls to be silent if they abuse or harass them.

LGBTQ+ rights

Over the last fifty years since the Stonewall riots, LGBTQ+ people have gained equal rights in many countries, such as being able to get married and become parents. However, there are still places where they experience violence, hate, and discrimination.

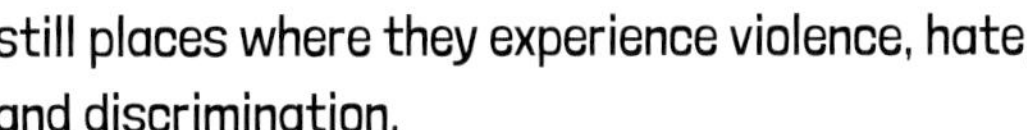

In Russia, the Church and government are **against LGBTQ+ people,** who often suffer physical and verbal attacks. LGBTQ+ activists have been arrested, beaten, and even killed—and many cities have banned Pride events.

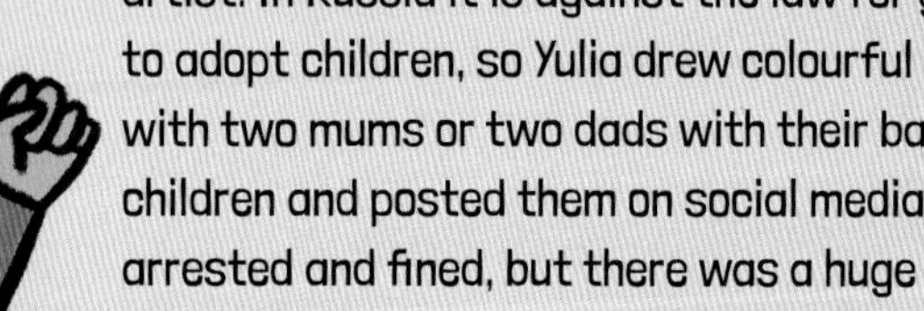

Yulia Tsvetkova is a Russian LGBTQ+ activist and artist. In Russia it is against the law for gay couples to adopt children, so Yulia drew colourful pictures with two mums or two dads with their babies and children and posted them on social media. She was arrested and fined, but there was a huge outcry and Yulia received support from celebrities, artists, and journalists in Russia and beyond.

ACTIVIST HERO

YULIA TSVETKOVA

Uses art to stand up for LGBTQ+ rights in Russia.

Yulia's poster says: 'Family is where love is Support LGBT+ families'

Protests from Yulia and other activists are **making a difference** in Russia. The government had

planned new laws to ban gay marriage and take away rights for transgender people, but these have been delayed and may be dropped completely. Public support for LGBTQ+ people in Russia is growing, especially among young people.

LGBTQ+ kids often get bullied for being different. American teenager Desmond Napoles has enjoyed wearing dresses, skirts, tutus, and make-up since he was 6 years old. Today Desmond is an LGBTQ+ activist who speaks up for LGBTQ+ children by giving talks and interviews, and has a huge social media following. He has written a children's book about Pride, released a song featuring other LGBTQ+ kids, and created safe and welcoming social networks for children and their parents. His motto is **'Be Yourself, Always'**.

ACTIVIST HERO

DESMOND NAPOLES

Speaks up for LGBTQ+ children.

Read on to find out about the activists working on the biggest issues affecting everyone today . . .

Chapter 7

Looking Forwards: Protest for the Planet

Humans are connected to all living things on earth.

The fossil fuels we use to power our homes and cars affect the entire planet, not just our local area. Trees in the Amazon rainforest absorb carbon from the atmosphere and produce life-giving oxygen for us all. And a virus jumping from animals to humans can spread quickly around the globe. Everyone in the world needs to come together to solve the planet's biggest problems. Children and young people are some of the loudest voices calling for change.

Climate change

Playing football is how Lesein Mutunkei plans to save the planet. When the teenager learned his country, Kenya, was losing the equivalent of **164 football pitches** of forest every day, and that tree-planting can help reverse climate change, he decided to make a difference by combining the two things he's most

passionate about—football and nature. He promised to plant a tree for every goal he scored, the start of his Trees4Goals initiative.

Football is an extremely popular sport, so Trees4Goals got lots of attention. When Lesein's friends wanted to join in he increased his pledge to **eleven trees per goal**—one for every member of the team. His school rugby and basketball clubs signed up too, and together they planted over 1,000 trees. Newspapers and television took notice, and soon the government agreed to provide Lesein with saplings.

Today Lesein dreams of a Trees4Goals forest in every country in Africa. His biggest hope is for **FIFA** to join in so that famous football players start planting trees too.

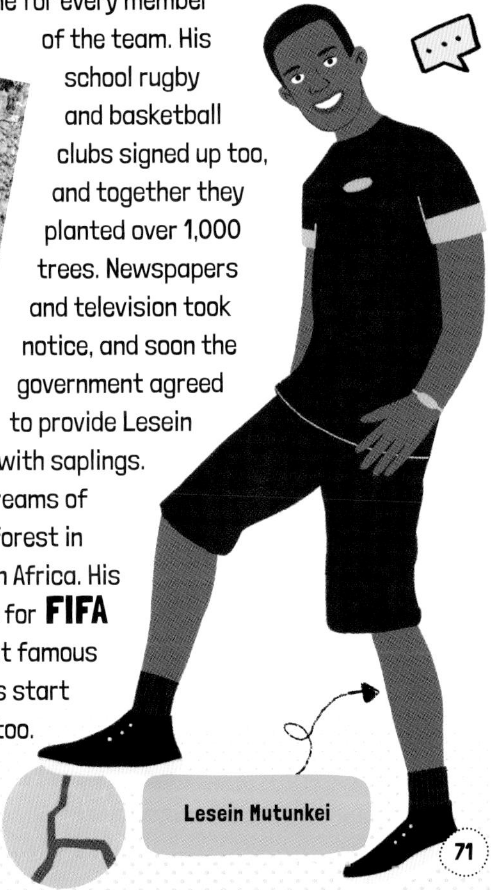

Lesein Mutunkei

ACTIVIST HERO

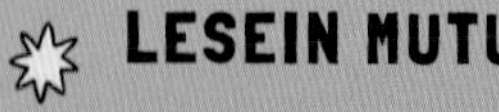

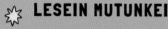

LESEIN MUTUNKEI

Started the Trees4Goals initiative.

Probably the most famous young climate activist is Greta Thunberg, who was 15 years old when she decided to organize a strike from school to protest about the Swedish government's inaction **against climate change.** A strike usually means workers refusing to work to try to get better pay, hours, and conditions, or in a general strike, people across a country stop working to try to force their government to make changes.

ACTIVIST HERO

GRETA THUNBERG

Started the Fridays for Future school strikes for the climate crisis.

Greta's school strike was inspired by the thousands of American students who took part in a school walk-out after a school shooter killed seventeen pupils at Marjory Stoneman Douglas High School in February 2018. Initially, no one wanted to join Greta's strike, so she started alone, sitting in front of Sweden's parliament building, but her solo action quickly grew to a **global movement**, with millions of young people from over 100 countries taking part. And today, Greta, once the quiet girl at the back of the class, is regularly invited to speak before huge crowds about climate change.

Inspiring young activists like Greta exist across the world—from Ou Hongyi, China's first climate striker, to the twenty-five young people in Colombia who took court action against the destruction of the Amazon rainforest in 2018. These activists argued for their right to grow up in a healthy environment, and the case was special because the court decided that **the Amazon rainforest has rights too**, like a human being. This idea is becoming important for protecting nature and the environment today, and it wouldn't have happened without the power of activism.

ACTIVIST HERO

SHEILA WATT-CLOUTIER

Climate justice activist for Inuit people.

Climate justice

Climate justice is the idea of climate change as a human rights issue as well as an environmental one. It is the understanding that the people who are least responsible for climate change are those who suffer worst from its effects.

Rich countries have produced most of the extra **carbon dioxide** in our atmosphere, which has caused sea ice to melt in the Arctic, among many other things. As well as impacting the homes of wildlife, this has meant that the Inuit (the indigenous people) have lost their traditional ways of life. Sheila Watt-Cloutier is an Inuit activist who **speaks up** for the rights of her people and has led efforts by using the law to **stop** other countries from polluting the atmosphere.

Over recent years, Australia has experienced **record-breaking temperatures** and devastating wildfires due to climate change. Some of those worst impacted have been Aboriginal and Torres Strait Islander peoples—the indigenous people of Australia who often live in poor communities as a result of unfair treatment after Australia became a British colony.

Amelia Telford was a teenager when she became a climate activist. She wanted to fight for the rights of Aboriginal and Torres Strait Islander peoples who had lost their land when Australia was colonized. Today she leads SEED—a youth group which **fights for climate justice** for first peoples of Australia and against the fossil fuel industry.

SEED activists believe in fun and creative tactics. Amelia protested against a new coal mine dressed as an orange-and-black clownfish from the film *Finding Nemo* to highlight the impact of fossil fuels on ocean life in the Great Barrier Reef. She even spoke to Australia's prime minister **dressed as Nemo!** SEED members also demonstrated outside a bank's headquarters, handing out roses to staff while asking them not to lend money to the new coal mine.

ACTIVIST HERO

AMELIA TELFORD

Climate justice activist for Aboriginal and Torres Strait Islander peoples.

Their colourful protests helped to stop some banks loaning money to the coal mine because they did not want negative publicity.

Ecological crisis

For ten days in April 2019, Extinction Rebellion (XR) caused severe disruption in London. Inspired by Gandhi and the US civil rights movement, XR activists are prepared to break the law but not to use violence. Protestors camped on bridges, others blocked busy roads, and some **glued themselves to the doors** of important buildings. People, young and old, demanded urgent action over the escalating ecological crisis.

XR poster. Many XR activists are willing to be arrested.

XR poster. XR activists demand urgent action over the ecological crisis.

There have been several mass extinctions in the history of planet Earth, including the one that wiped out the dinosaurs. Today, we're undergoing another mass extinction, with species dying out every day, but this one is mostly caused by humans.

Our need for land for towns, cities, and farming lifestock has squeezed out wildlife. Today, people and our pets and farm animals make up **96%** of all mammals on Earth, while **70%** of birds are chickens because of human demand for chicken to eat. Wildlife habitats are further threatened by climate change, mining, deforestation, roads, and railways. Pollution is harming rivers and oceans. We urgently need to find a way to share our planet with nature. XR's protests have helped make many governments declare a climate emergency.

ACTIVIST HERO

ROK ROZMAN

Kayaks to protect wild rivers.

There are lots of ways to defend nature. Slovenian kayaker Rok Rozman and his friends paddled twenty-three rivers in the Balkans to protest against new dams which would destroy river wildlife. In Bali, sisters Isabel and Melati Wijsen created a youth-led charity, Bye Bye Plastic Bags, and their online petition resulted in the ban of single-use plastics from their country. And around the globe each year, thousands of people take part in the **World Naked Bike Ride** to promote cycling as a greener way to travel!

ACTIVIST HEROES

ISABEL AND MELATI WIJSEN

Sisters who set up Bye Bye Plastic Bags.

Animal rights

Texas, USA, is home to cattle ranches and rodeos and, surprisingly, a farm animal sanctuary where cows, ducks, hens, and pigs live out their lives in peace. The sanctuary was created by Renee King-Sonnen, who became vegan after raising a calf named Rowdy Girl and getting to know the other cows on her husband Tommy's ranch. She eventually persuaded Tommy to become vegan too and they converted the ranch into **Rowdy Girl Sanctuary.** Renee and Tommy are vegan activists who try to change people's minds by example.

Most animal rights activists think that animals should not be used for experiments and that they should not be bred or killed for food, clothing, or medicines. Animal-rights campaigners believe that if humans have rights then non-human

ACTIVIST HERO

RENEE KING-SONNEN

Runs Rowdy Girl Sanctuary and campaigns for veganism.

animals should have rights too. Many campaigners also believe that it is wrong to hunt animals, to keep them in zoos, or to use them for entertainment.

Animal-rights activists have used many methods to bring about change. Some make films about life in factory farms for animals like pigs and chickens. The film *Blackfish* showed the story of an **orca in captivity** and helped to end orca shows at SeaWorld™. Some activists use extreme methods to make their point, such as freeing animals from laboratories or throwing paint on people wearing fur at fashion shows.

Through their campaigns, activists have changed the way many people view animals. Increasing numbers of people have stopped eating meat and today many companies have **stopped experimenting on animals**. Singer Billie Eilish agreed to wear a designer dress to a snazzy event as long as the brand went fur-free. **And they did!**

Poverty and inequality

Poverty means a life of struggle. In some countries, schools aren't free of charge, and not all families can afford to send their children to school. They might also need them to work and earn money for the family. Some families can't afford to get medical treatment. In countries where people lack access to clean water and proper toilets, poverty means the spread of preventable diseases that can kill people, especially children.

Nelson Mandela, the first Black president of South Africa and anti-apartheid activist, believed that extreme poverty could be overcome, just like slavery and apartheid. In 2005, the Make Poverty History movement involved campaigns, concerts, and marches in many countries and, following this, the UN set the goal to eradicate extreme poverty by 2030.

MAKEPOVERTYHISTORY

Nelson Mandela speaking at a Make Poverty History march

There have been **huge** improvements in the last thirty years.

Estimates in 2019 showed that 9.2% of the world, or 689 million people, lived in extreme poverty on $1.90 or less a day, compared to 36% in 1990. But since 2020, the COVID-19 pandemic has plunged millions more into poverty, because people have lost their jobs and opportunities to complete their education. This is the first time since 1998 that **poverty has increased.**

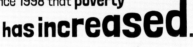

Even in richer countries, there are people living in **'relative poverty'**, which means they are poor compared to most people in the country and often unable to afford essentials like food. During the pandemic, Manchester United football player Marcus Rashford campaigned for children in England who would have received free meals at school to continue to get them while schools were closed under lockdown.

Marcus Rashford MBE and mum Melanie visiting a charity in Manchester

When Marcus was growing up there wasn't always enough food, despite his hardworking mum's best efforts, and he believes that no child should go to bed hungry. He wrote to politicians, appeared on television and radio, spoke out using social media, and created an online petition with **over a million signatures**. His campaigning succeeded and the government agreed to extend free school meal vouchers through school holidays.

ACTIVIST HERO

MARCUS RASHFORD

Footballer who campaigns to end child poverty in England.

Most people believe inequality is wrong. The global Occupy Movement, formed in America in 2011, campaigns against the huge gap between rich and poor people, and the power of big companies. 'Occupy' formed part of the 'global justice movement', which uses the slogan **'We are the 99%'**,

highlighting the fact that the combined wealth America's richest 1% is much greater than the combined wealth of the rest of the population—the remaining 99%. This great slogan sums up a **shocking** fact that most people probably don't realize—that a small group of extremely wealthy people rule the world. Catchy slogans make it easy to highlight a cause and tell people what it's about in a memorable way.

Migrants, asylum seekers, and refugees

Migrants and **refugees** are **not always welcomed** in the countries they arrive in because of racism, or people's fears that the new arrivals might take their jobs and change their communities. In 2018, in America, the president, Donald Trump ruled that migrants and **asylum seekers** arriving at the US border should be imprisoned before being **deported** (sent back to the country they came from). Furthermore, it is estimated that **over 5,000 non-US-citizen** children were separated from their parents and sent to live with foster parents or in **detention centres.** Even though this cruel practice has stopped, many of those children may never be reunited with their families.

Speak like an activist

MIGRANT

A migrant is someone who chooses to move to another country to improve their life, for example by finding better work, or to escape poverty.

REFUGEE

A refugee is someone who has been forced to leave their home or country to escape a natural disaster, war, or persecution (being treated badly, especially due to their race, political, or religious beliefs), and would be in danger if they returned.

ASYLUM SEEKER

An asylum seeker is someone who has applied for protection as a refugee.

While governments might want to drive away migrants, the communities they live in don't necessarily agree—and they can make a difference. On the morning of 13th May 2021, there was a raid on a house in Glasgow, Scotland, by government immigration officers.

Two men from India were bundled into a van to take them to a detention centre before being deported. But when their neighbours saw what was happening, they rushed on to the street and surrounded the van to stop it leaving. One man even lay beneath it, next to the wheels. Thanks to the ***lightning speed*** of social media, the protest soon swelled to hundreds of people filling the road and chanting.

These are our neighbours, let them go!

The people united will never be defeated!

IMMIGRATION ENFORCEMENT

The chant 'The people united shall never be defeated' has been made popular by many protest movements, and originally came from a Chilean protest song, *El Pueblo Unido Jamás Será Vencido*, before becoming a Chilean chant for social justice. Chants and songs are an important tool in activism to help people get their voices heard and to spread powerful messages. They give demonstrations more power, impact, and energy.

After eight hours of peaceful but noisy protest, the men were eventually set free by police. Just like the famous chant, that day in Glasgow people united to protest about the treatment of immigrants in a completely unplanned way—and won. **That's the amazing power of activism!**

ACTIVIST HEROES

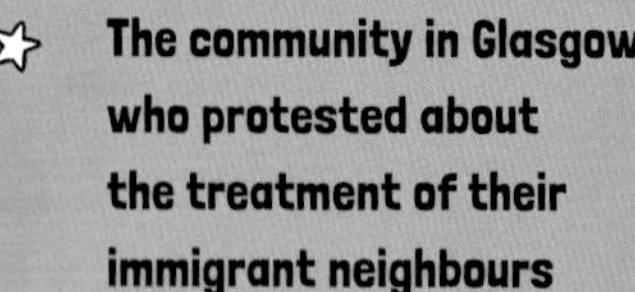

- **The community in Glasgow who protested about the treatment of their immigrant neighbours**

Chapter 8

The Future of Activism

Humans have a unique ability to co-operate and collaborate. This makes us capable of amazing things.

As we've seen throughout this book, change happens when people come together to **fight for what they believe in,** and many of the freedoms and rights we enjoy today are thanks to those activists of the past. Individual actions count too. Greta Thunberg and Rosa Parks show us that the solo act of sitting down can spark a world-changing movement. In fact, there are so many examples of **amazing** activism that it was difficult to choose what to write about, and there are countless others that could have been included in this book.

Humans can be both good and bad.

There has always been injustice and people have always disagreed, so there will always be activism and protest. People will continue to make their voices heard when they're not represented, or when they feel that their leaders aren't talking about and changing the right things.

The **COVID-19 pandemic**, which began in 2019, shone a light on many issues around the world: poverty and inequality, unequal access to vaccines, the destruction of nature, loneliness and mental health. And many activists are already trying to tackle these problems.

The pandemic also meant that activists couldn't meet in groups. Instead they were forced to go online through video calls, petitions, social media, and blogging. These methods are here to stay, alongside traditional tactics, because they are the quickest ways to spread ideas and get support for a cause, and people can take part wherever they are in the world. This will be important since many of our **biggest** problems are global ones.

The climate crisis is likely to stay at the forefront of activism because it's a long way from being solved. Its effects—including mass migration and conflicts over resources like land and water—will trigger other issues for us to face. People will take action through activism to have their say on these subjects.

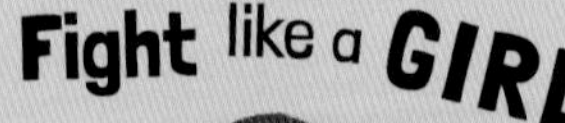

Many of the change-makers fighting for our planet are young people just like you.

Are you an eco-warrior?

Maybe you're standing up for wildlife, planting trees, or cleaning up beaches?

Or is there something else that you're passionate about?

Perhaps **you'll** use the amazing power of activism in the future, too.

Go change THE WORLD!

Glossary

abolitionist someone who campaigns for the ending of a particular system or way

asylum seeker a person who has been forced to leave their home country for their own safety and has asked to be allowed to live in another country

boycott refuse to buy a product as a protest

campaign a plan of activities to help bring about or prevent a change in society

civil disobedience a refusal to obey certain laws and demands of a government as a protest

civil rights people's rights, given by their government, to vote for their leaders, to buy a home, or be educated

climate justice the understanding that climate change has the biggest effect on people who are the least responsible for it, and often less well-off, and this makes it a human rights issue not just an environmental one

democracy a system of government where people vote for people to represent them and their wishes

demonstration a march or gathering of people to protest against something or express opinions on an issue

deport make a person leave a country because they have committed a crime or the government believes they are not allowed to live in that country

detention centre where people who have come into a country illegally are detained while a decision is made about whether they can stay in that country

dictatorship a system where political power is held by a single person, other political parties are not allowed, and people have little freedom to say what they want

discrimination when a person or group is treated less fairly than other people or groups

feminism the belief and aim that women should have the same rights, power, and opportunities as men, formerly known as women's liberation

feudal system the system in the Middle Ages in which nobles were given land by the king in exchange for military service. Most people

worked for the nobles, and poor farmers, or serfs lived on the land, farmed it, and paid the nobles for it. Serfs could be sold with the land too

guerrilla an armed resistance fighter

human rights rights that everyone has because they are humans, including the right to freedom, shelter, and food, and not to be treated badly

hunger strike when someone refuses to eat, usually for days or even weeks, as a protest

immigrant a person who comes to live permanently in another country

indigenous originally coming from a particular place

LGBTQ+ stands for lesbian, gay, bisexual, transgender, queer, questioning, and ace

migrant a person who moves from one place to another to find work or better living conditions

mutiny a rebellion against the authorities, especially by soldiers or sailors against their officers

Nobel Peace Prize an award given each year to someone who has done important work for world peace

oppression unfair, unjust, or cruel treatment by authorities or rulers

petition a document, usually signed by lots of people, which asks a government or other authority to do, or not do, a particular thing

police brutality extreme physical violence by police

politics activities to do with organizing and running countries or other groups of people

protest an organized demonstration to show that people disapprove of something

racial justice fair treatment of everyone, regardless of their ethnicity

racism the belief that one race is naturally superior to another

rally a large meeting to show support for something

rebellion the act of resisting authority, sometimes through violence

reconciliation bringing people together to help them understand their differences

refugee a person who has been forced to leave their home or country to escape a natural disaster, war, or persecution

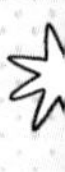

resistance the refusal to accept something, or the use of force to oppose someone or something

revolt an attempt by a group of people to change their country's political system

revolution when a government or authority is removed from power, often by masses of people rebelling against unfair rule

sabotage damaging or destroying something on purpose to put a person or organization at a disadvantage

segregation a system of laws which separate humans, e.g. according to their race or gender, and keep them apart, often with the result that one group suffers

sit-in a protest where people go to a place and refuse to leave it until their demands are met

social movement an organized effort by a large group of people to achieve a particular goal, usually a social or political one. This may be to make, resist, or undo a social change

strike a refusal to work or go to school as a protest

trade union an organized group of workers who join together to negotiate pay, hours, benefits, and working conditions

United Nations (UN)
An international group of countries, formed in 1945, which aims to promote peace and security in the world, establish friendly relations between its members, support human rights, and make sure countries follow international laws

uprising a violent organized action by a group of people

working class the group of people in a society who do not own much property, who have low social status, and many of whom do jobs involving physical skills

Index